Unauthorized Portraits

Edward Sorel

Unauthorized Portraits

Alfred A. Knopf New York 1997

THIS IS A BORZOI BOOK
PUBLISHED BY ALFRED A. KNOPF, INC.

Copyright © 1997 by Edward Sorel
All rights reserved under International and Pan-American Copyright
Conventions. Published in the United States by Alfred A. Knopf, Inc.,
New York, and simultaneously in Canada by Random House of Canada
Limited, Toronto. Distributed by Random House, Inc., New York.

http://www.randomhouse.com/

Library of Congress Cataloging-in-Publication Data
Sorel, Edward, [date]
Unauthorized portraits / Edward Sorel.
p.   cm.
ISBN 0-679-45466-7
1. Celebrities—Caricatures and cartoons. 2. American wit
and humor, Pictorial. I. Title.
NC1429.S568A4   1997
741.5'973—dc21   97-7691   CIP

Manufactured in Italy
First Edition

Frontispiece illustration from the cover of The New Yorker, *January 31, 1994.*

For Nancy

Acknowledgments

O NCE AGAIN I am grateful to my good friend Marcus Ratliff for designing another one of my books. Somehow his quiet approach to book design always seems perfect to me. His assistant, Amy Pyle, performed her usual graphic magic on the computer.

Also deserving a low bow is my editor, Ann Close, whose certitude about which drawings were worthy and which not made life easy for a cartoonist given to vacillation. And another bow to Romeo Enriquez, for his devotion to excellence in production. Other shoulders I leaned on at Knopf were those of my longtime friends Katherine Hourigan, Anthea Lingeman, and Nina Bourne, each of whom contributed her particular expertise to this book.

Thanks also to those editors and art directors who originally commissioned the work collected here: Walter Bernard, Peter Bloch, Tina Brown, Art Cooper, Chris Curry, Byron Dobell, Clay Felker, Milton Glaser, Andy Kner, Richard Lingeman, George Lois, Lee Lorenz, Robert Manning, Françoise Mouly, Victor Navasky, Richard Snow, Francis Tanabe, William Whitworth, and Shelley Zalaznick. Without them there would be no book. I tip my hat to Hugh Hefner for retrieving much-needed art, and to the good people at the New York Public Library Picture Collection who always found the reference I needed.

A final nod goes to Irene Skolnick—good agent, good company—who has ruined her eyes reading the very small type in my contracts.

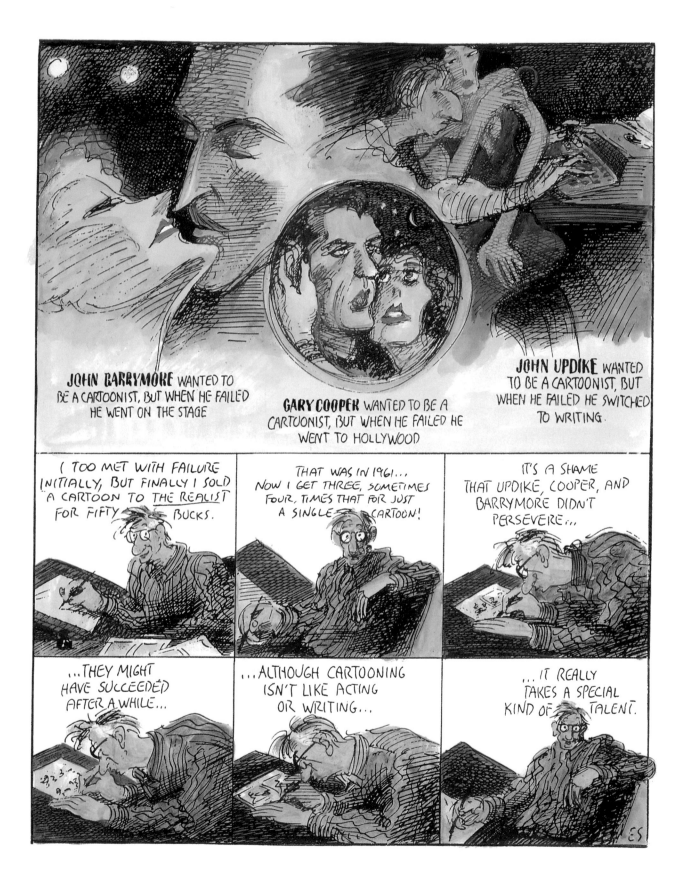

Introduction

C ONTRARY TO WHAT we've been led to believe, the unexamined life *is* worth living. In fact, if you've decided to devote your life to drawing comic portraits that are deliberately hurtful, the last thing you want to do is examine your inner self.

In my own defense, I must protest that I never planned to be a caricaturist. My earliest works of art, far from being cruel or belittling, were upbeat and worshipful. Consider my first printed drawing, done in 1943, when I was in the eighth grade at P.S. 90. Not only is it optimistic, it's downright patriotic—that "V" in the background is for "Victory."

Cynicism started to creep into my work when I attended the High School of Music and Art. There, instead of learning how to improve my drawing, I was encouraged to concentrate on abstract design—an aesthetic that has never held the slightest interest for me. Cooper Union's art school was no better. In painting class there was no instruction about method, for fear of inhibiting our creative impulses. If I was going to learn how to draw, it would have to be someplace other than art school.

That place turned out to be a large cold-water loft with a kerosene heater that periodically caught fire. It was the first home of Push Pin Studios, an enterprise whose beginning still seems remarkable to me. In 1953, two years after Seymour Chwast and I graduated from Cooper Union, we found ourselves working at *Esquire* magazine and bored silly. We decided to seek out freelance work while still on staff. Our vehicle was to be a four-page, illustrated promotion piece that parodied old almanacs, called *The Push Pin Almanack.* It fit into a No. 10 envelope and was sent to hundreds of art directors. We hoped we would at least get enough work to pay for our postage.

We did—and considerably more. Seymour got most of the jobs. Somehow, even after three years at Cooper Union, he could still draw. I, on the

I was fourteen in 1943, too young to join up, but I boosted morale on the home front by drawing Columbia victorious against Stupidity, War, and Tyranny. I solved the difficult problem of how to draw ears by pretending they didn't exist.

OPPOSITE:
My long association with *Penthouse* was unique. They bought every idea I submitted to them, and never changed anything except my spelling. This solipsistic strip appeared in 1990.

After I graduated from Cooper Union, I no longer knew how to draw, and illustrated this first issue of *The Push Pin Almanack* in the flat cubist style all students were required to learn.

other hand, could now only do the kind of two-dimensional design that had been drilled into me. Seymour and I spoke about the possibility of devoting full time to an art studio, but it seemed too risky. He had a wife to support, and we had no sustaining clients. Then something wonderful happened: we both got fired, and on the same day. Fate had dictated we take a chance. We told the phone company that in addition to the coin-operated phone we had on our wall, we wanted a private phone installed. We were in business!

Some months later, when our classmate Milton Glaser returned from his Fulbright year in Italy, our duo became a trio. Then the studio really took off. The three of us put in sixteen-hour days turning out record album covers, book jackets, letterheads, and anything that came our way. Best of all, largely from watching Milton and Seymour, I was learning how to draw again—although I have to admit that my style was heavily influenced by theirs.

After two years I decided to see what I could do on my own. I left Push Pin on the very day the studio moved from the loft to plush quarters on the fashionable East Side. Some friends accused me of having a "poverty wish." Perhaps I did, but there really were things I could do on my own. A children's book, for one thing. My version of Charles Perrault's "Riquet with the Tuft of Hair," which I called *King Carlo of Capri,* was hardly a monetary success, but it was a turning point. All the pen-and-ink illustrations were done without any tracing or light box or pencil indication. They were done "direct"—an extremely eccentric thing to do in pen and ink. One mistake and you have to start all over. Starting over—and over and over—is something I'm used to by now, but in 1960 it was all quite new to me. When the book was included in the *New York Times* list of ten best illustrated books, I felt I was on to something.

As you can see, I had no particular interest in caricature, and the few times I had tried it, no gift for it. Few of my frequent magazine assignments required caricature. At that time Victor Navasky was publishing a political humor magazine called *Monocle*. He had no money and needed an art director; I had no money and needed a place to work. I moved my drawing board into *Monocle*'s mayhem. What I didn't realize was that Victor not only had no money to pay me, but he had no money to pay anyone. Oddly enough, he didn't need to. First-rate artists like Tomi Ungerer, David Levine, and Ed Koren (all young then) were eager to get their political art printed somewhere, and agreed to contribute. Still, there were other pages that required illustration—preferably caricatures—and I was the only one around to provide them. It turned out to be good practice. President Kennedy had just begun sending advisers to Vietnam.

Vietnam, of course, changed everything. Magazines that had previously shunned even the mildest satiric comment

My first movie-poster parody appeared in *The Realist* in 1961. Since Robert Kennedy had sired nine children, I assumed he was using the rhythm method of birth control.

were urging me to "let loose." *Esquire*, a far different magazine than the one that had fired me ten years before, was assigning me the caricatures that David Levine was too busy to accept. I began to do a monthly page for a new magazine called *Ramparts*, a left-wing, full-color periodical published in San Francisco. "Sorel's Bestiary" caricatured politicians as the beasts they most resembled: Bobby Kennedy as a "varying hare," for example, and LBJ as a crocodile. The drawing was uneven in quality, but people were hungry for protest art and gobbled up whatever I did.

I had occasionally worked for the *Herald Tribune*'s Sunday supplement, *New York*, and when it became a newsstand magazine in 1968, with Clay Felker as editor and my former partner Milton Glaser as art director, I found myself listed on the masthead as a contributing editor. It was in *New York* that many of my early political satires appeared; one issue was entirely illustrated

I usually do finished sketches before submitting an idea for a book jacket, but I was so certain this idea—a chorus line of naked statesmen with missiles for penises—would be rejected that I did only a quick rough. The publisher bought it. (See page 116.)

by me. A few years later Felker bought the *Village Voice* and gave me space for a regular feature. (This brought me only a page away from my unsuspecting mentor, Jules Feiffer, whose weekly cartoon taught me to forget the traditional comic-strip balloon and let the words float free.) Tight deadlines for both these publications required me to work fast and had a liberating effect on my style. My drawings were getting freer, more spontaneous. For the first time I was beginning to like my own work—I was beginning to understand what Degas meant by "premeditated spontaneity."

My caricatures, too, were getting bolder. Not as bold as I wished them to be, not as bold as those of Feliks Topolski, the British draftsman and caricaturist whom I admired above all others, but at least they were less timid. By the end of the 1960s my metamorphosis from decorative illustrator to caricaturist was complete, and at a time when the demand for caricaturists far exceeded the supply. Magazines had become news-oriented, personality-focused, creating a need for caricature to liven up the page. David Levine had proved the value of caricature in the pages of the *New York Review of Books,* and other periodicals took note. During the 1970s my caricatures appeared on the covers of *Ramparts, Esquire,* the *Atlantic Monthly, Harper's,* the *Columbia Journalism Review,* the *Evergreen Review, Forbes, Fortune,* the *National Lampoon, Rolling Stone, Screw, Sports Illustrated, New York, The Nation,* and *Time.*

Few of those covers are in this book. Many embarrass me now; it has always been hard for me to do a good drawing unless I'm excited by the idea or passionate about the subject. Boredom shows. By the end of the decade the thought of caricaturing yet another politician exhausted me before I began. Wanting an escape from the ephemeral character of politics, I embarked on "First Encounters" with my wife, Nancy, for the *Atlantic Monthly.* The nature of that series—real accounts of the initial meetings of historical personages—forced me into a more nuanced approach than was possible with caricatures having no setting or narrative. In short, it forced me into doing some of my best drawings. Most of these illustrations have already been published in our book *First Encounters* (Knopf, 1994), but those that appeared after the book went to press are included here.

A digression. In all the fourteen years Nancy and I did "First Encounters" for the *Atlantic,* editor William Whitworth never second-guessed our choices or asked for changes—except once. The illustration for the meeting between Freud and Mahler shows them walking along the streets of Leyden, Holland, where the composer had gone to seek help from the vacationing psychoanalyst. Mahler had been suffering from impotence, and as both were cigar smokers, I hit upon the (brilliant) idea of drawing Freud's cigar large and erect and Mahler's small and limp. In Boston Whitworth viewed these cigars with grave misgiving and sent the drawing back by courier for immediate alteration (just as Nancy had said he would).

Although it's true that, politically, I dozed through the Carter years, by Reagan's second term my sense of outrage had been nudged awake. I began submitting cartoon strips on the political scene to *The Nation,* where the editor was none other than my old *Monocle* boss, Victor Navasky. I found him as parsimonious as ever, and took my revenge by occasionally slipping in a strip

AFTER THE CAMERA intruded itself into the nineteenth century, artists who once were assigned to paint historic moments found themselves contending with a mechanical device that could capture a crowd at a coronation in less than a second. How could an artist compete? Obviously, by doing things the camera can't. Even after a century and a half of improvements, the camera remains hopeless for noncontemporaneous events. Perhaps that's why I'm drawn to history: photographers can't get there.

I enjoy historical research. It has taught me that the truth about much-lauded events of the past lies in the footnotes. The Boston Tea Party, for example, made a lot more sense once I read the six-point type which explained that John Hancock had bribed waterfront hoodlums to dump the British tea because he had a warehouse full of the Dutch variety. Then there was Gilbert Stuart's portrait of George Washington. Seems that Martha had commissioned the portrait, but every time the first President asked for it, he was told it wasn't quite finished. This was true—Stuart intentionally left one area incomplete. But his unwillingness to let the painting leave his studio was because he was busy producing copies—seventy in all—which he sold for $100 each, big bucks then. It was a cottage industry successful beyond all expectation.

It's those footnotes that led me down the path to cynicism. But there are worse destinies. In *The Devil's Dictionary*, Ambrose Bierce defined a cynic as "a blackguard whose faulty vision sees things as they are, not as they ought to be." It's not always easy to discover how things really are, but I continue to try.

A preemptive apology: Early on in these pages there's a strip in which God complains about the heavy burdens of his office. Clearly, God does not belong in a "history" section. The problem is that God is difficult to fit into any category (as well as being impossible to shop for) and I had to put him somewhere. Everything else that I allege happened actually did.

OPPOSITE:
Cover illustration for an article explaining how computers are now employed by biblical scholars. Substituting printouts for tablets occurred to me as an effective way to get the idea across, but like most graphic allegories, it doesn't bear close scrutiny. Gustave Doré inspired my Moses. "Translating the Bible: An Endless Task," *Atlantic Monthly,* February 1985.

Nebuchadnezzar, king of Babylonia (c. 605–562 B.C.), piqued at an insufficiency of taxes collected from the Hebrews by Zedekiah, beheads Zedekiah's sons in front of him, then gouges out his eyes. From my pictorial essay "A Short-Form History of Taxation," *GQ*, March 1996.

OPPOSITE:
Exodus revisited: an educated guess as to what Moses endured as he led his people through the Red Sea. A cartoon for *Penthouse*, the only mass-circulation magazine to welcome my blasphemy, April 1995.

At work in his laboratory, Bolognese professor of anatomy
Luigi Galvani accidentally grazes a knife against a machine producing charges of static electricity, then touches the knife to a
dismembered frog. He is amazed to see it twitch. Although his
eventual conclusion—that such spasmodic movement is caused
by "animal electricity"—is proved wrong, the connection remains, and today we are "galvanized" into action. *Word People.*

OPPOSITE:
Madame de Pompadour, beautiful and accomplished mistress
to King Louis XV, pretends not to notice the shadowy figure
of Monsieur Etienne de Silhouette, controller-general of
France, whose stringent economies reined in her extravagance.
He lasts eight months; she, twenty years; their names, forever.
Word People.

A poor young man of twenty, Johannes Brahms makes his way
to Weimar to visit Franz Liszt. When Brahms is too shy to play
his Scherzo in E-flat minor, the master performs it for him, then
moves on to his own works. But the day is warm, the air close,
and the young Johannes weary from his journey. Not even the
impassioned chords of Liszt's B minor Sonata can save him.
Illustration for "First Encounters" by Nancy Caldwell Sorel in
the *Atlantic Monthly*, May 1994.

OPPOSITE:
Tenor Enrico Caruso is a guest at the St. Francis Hotel when
the 1906 earthquake strikes San Francisco. He vows *never* to
return to a city "where things like this are permitted." From my
pictorial essay "Keyhole History," *GQ*, October 1984.

English painter Gwen John, age twenty-seven, applied for a modeling job at the studio of Auguste Rodin, sixty-three. The sculptor declared she had *un corps admirable,* and she was hired. One thing led to another. . . . "First Encounters," *Atlantic Monthly,* November 1994.

Mrs. Stuyvesant Fish, on the morning after one of her glittering parties, opened the New York *Herald* to discover that her guest list had been switched with the names of those who held ringside seats at the previous night's prizefight. OPPOSITE: In 1871 James Butler ("Wild Bill") Hickok, marshal of Abilene, was playing poker one night in the Alamo saloon when he heard gunshots in the street. Furious at the interruption, he rushed into the darkness and shot an innocent bystander, after which, hearing someone behind him, he spun around and killed his own deputy. "Footnotes to History," *American Heritage,* February 1990.

Henry R. Luce, at a party on the Starlight Roof of the Waldorf-Astoria, is carrying champagne to his wife when he is waylaid by the beautiful Clare Boothe Brokaw. Is it possible, she asks, that the champagne is for her? A lengthy conversation follows, at the end of which the head of Time Inc. informs his new friend that he intends to marry her. Illustration for "Divorce Deco" by Nancy Caldwell Sorel, *Esquire,* November 1983.

While president of Prince-
ton, Woodrow Wilson
opened the morning paper
to headlines quoting him as
saying that "Chewing To-
bacco Makes Men Think."
His actual words (in a
speech the day before) were
that "the habit of chewing
tobacco . . . makes men
think because they must
stop between words to spit."
Illustration for "The Press"
by Peter Andrews, *American
Heritage,* October 1994.

OPPOSITE:
Mr. and Mrs. Jimmy Walker
outside a polling booth in
November 1925. Why is he
so cheerful? He knows he
will be elected mayor of
New York, he's wise as to
how to get rich on the job,
and he has a pretty mistress
in Hollywood. Illustration
for "1925: The Year It All
Began," *The New Yorker,*
February 20, 1995

Appointed secretary of the treasury in 1921, Andrew Mellon declared that his first priority was to "simplify" taxes. His method involved slashing the tax rate for America's rich from 73 to 25 percent and expanding the oil depletion allowance for his friends in the petroleum industry. "A Short-Form History of Taxation," *GQ.* March 1996.

OPPOSITE:
In 1942 Frank Lloyd Wright was summoned to the White House to discuss housing for the Oak Ridge, Tennessee, atomic bomb plant with FDR. But Wright was a more practiced critic than consultant. "Frank," he boomed at the President, "you ought to get up out of that chair and look around at what they're doing to your city here, miles and miles of Ionic and Corinthian columns." The contract for Oak Ridge went elsewhere. "Footnotes to History," *American Heritage,* February 1990.

When a sex scandal eliminated Gary Hart as a presidential candidate, our past presidents were placed under scrutiny by writer Sidney Blumenthal. My illustration focuses on the most recognizable figures, but in fact the only president Blumenthal certified to be without carnal sin was Richard Nixon. From "Oval Office Sex," *GQ*, November 1987.

Terence Cardinal Cooke is informed of President Kennedy's White House shenanigans. The prelate comforts Cooke: "After all, there is no evidence to suggest he was practicing unnatural methods of birth control." *Penthouse,* January 1977.

OPPOSITE:
"How Was I Supposed to Know?" *The Nation,* September 24, 1990.

1945 RESIDENTS OF BUCHENWALD ARE SHOCKED TO LEARN THAT EXTERMINATION CAMPS EXISTED IN THEIR TOWN.

1972 NIXON IS SHOCKED TO LEARN WHITE HOUSE STAFFERS WERE INVOLVED IN WATERGATE.

1986 RONALD REAGAN IS SHOCKED TO LEARN THAT MEMBERS OF HIS STAFF SOLD ARMS TO IRAN.

1990 BUSH IS SHOCKED! THE NICE MAN HE SOLD ARMS TO TURNS OUT TO BE A LUNATIC, AND HAS INVADED KUWAII.

During the period of protest against the war in Vietnam, there was a withdrawal from science. Astrology came to the fore. I had little patience with otherwise rational people taking it seriously, and mocked their credulity by gathering together disparate types born under the same sign. The "doctors" here were all born under the constellation Leo. Andy Warhol, James Baldwin, George Meany, Stanley Kubrick, and Alfred Hitchcock watch as Fidel Castro dissects a corpse in a takeoff on Rembrandt's *The Anatomy Lesson*. This and several following are from my "Celebrity Astrology" series in *Audience* magazine. July–August 1972.

A sixteenth-century hunting scene is populated by men (no Dianas here) born under the sign of Capricorn and therefore conventional, devoted careerists, always on the lookout for a new opportunity. With Edward Teller as canine and Howard Hughes as unicorn, Wilfrid Sheed, I. F. Stone, Richard Nixon, and Julian Bond set off after their prey. *Audience,* January–February 1972.

Getting back to nature in the manner of Manet are Taureans Barbra Streisand, Robert Andrew Parker, Vladimir Nabokov, Bernadette Devlin, Duke Ellington, and Edmund Wilson. *Audience,* May–June 1972.

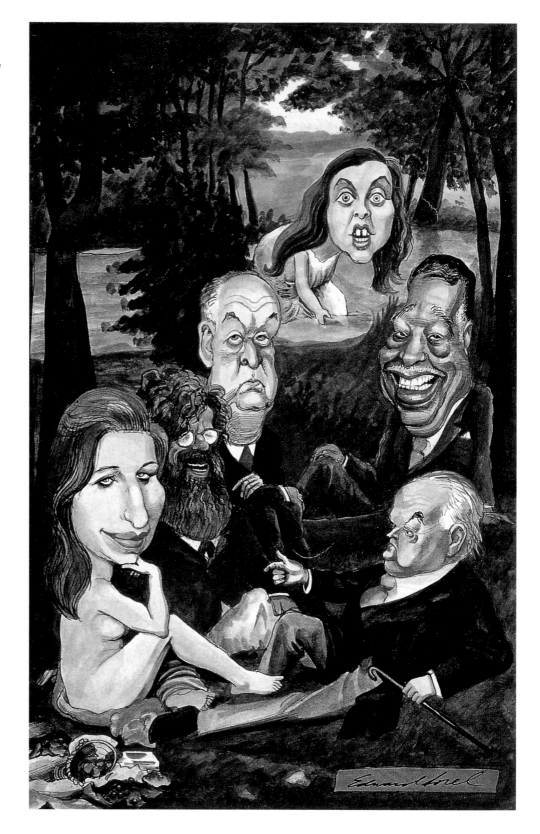

Inconsistency is the worst trait of those born under the sign of Gemini, and their tendency to flirt comes from their inherent need for dual relationships. Frolicking in a Watteau-like landscape are Clint Eastwood, Henry Kissinger, David Rockefeller, Joyce Carol Oates, Norman Vincent Peale, and Hubert Humphrey. *Audience,* May–June 1972.

John James Audubon, long-haired American backwoodsman fresh off the cotton packet with his portfolio of precious bird drawings, visits Edinburgh and is struck speechless with awe in the presence of the great Sir Walter Scott. The novelist, for his part, cares nothing about ornithology, but knows hero material when he sees it. "First Encounters," *Atlantic Monthly,* March 1994.

John Ruskin escapes in horror from his marriage bed when he discovers that his bride, Euphemia Gray—unlike the marble statues of his beloved Greeks—has pubic hair. Unpublished.

OPPOSITE:
If Nora Ephron's novel *Heartburn* is to be taken as a roman à clef, then husband Carl Bernstein's roving eye made monogamy impossible. Illustration for "Love Among the Literati" by Nancy Caldwell Sorel, *GQ* June 1985.

Eight months into an already shaky marriage, Joe DiMaggio followed Marilyn Monroe to New York, where, much against his wishes, she was scheduled to film location shots for *The Seven Year Itch*. The skirt-blowing over a subway grate was a tricky scene, and as retake followed retake and more and more sidewalk onlookers ogled his wife's white panties, Joe's fury increased. In time he stalked off, convinced the marriage was over—which it soon was. "Let's Call the Whole Thing Off," *GQ*, July 1988.

OPPOSITE:

The Burton-Taylor romance that inspired this pseudo-poster always seemed more like screwball comedy than real life. Few fans will remember Henry Wynberg; he was the eager suitor Liz dumped to marry Dick for the second time. Edgar Kennedy was the movie comedian famous for his "slow burn," *Village Voice*, August 1975.

NOTHING WILL reveal my middlebrow intellect so nakedly as this section—supposedly devoted to art, literature, dance, and drama—but almost entirely about movies. Movies are my real passion. My wife finds it disconcerting that I dream about Lilli Palmer or Dorothy McGuire and never about her.

Two pictures in this section—both to do with movies—almost undid me. One, "The Warner Mob," was done for a magazine that David Levine, Walter Bernard, and I tried to start in the late 1970s. We called it the *New York Film Review,* and got our friends Byron Dobell (editor of *American Heritage*) and Shelley Zalaznick (managing editor of *Forbes*) to give us a hand on our dummy issue. I was assigned the center spread. The fear of being compared to the incomparable David, who was doing the cover, paralyzed me for months. By the time our fledgling magazine was complete, interest rates were well into double digits, and potential investors kept their cash in the bank. The *Film Review* did not fly, and we never returned to it.

The other illustration that almost sent me over the edge was the one I did to accompany my article on the making of the film *Casablanca.* It was the largest picture I had ever undertaken (40" x 60"), and only the second time I had attempted a pastel. Another difficulty was that the movie was so dear to me: I know it's rife with Hollywood clichés, but I wanted to pay it homage anyway. Some have suggested that the reason for its enduring hold on audiences is the warm familiarity of its plot and characters from previous films. The late Lincoln Kirstein put it this way: "Two clichés make us laugh but a hundred clichés move us because we sense dimly that the clichés are talking among themselves, celebrating a reunion."

Most movies caricatured in this section are movies I remember vividly from my youth. Gathering them together here is something of a reunion for me.

OPPOSITE:
Cover, "The Melting Plot," for the summer fiction issue of *The New Yorker,* July 4, 1994. America makes no distinction between high and low art, only between success and failure.

The 1973 Academy Awards are remembered for Marlon
Brando's refusal to accept his Oscar for *The Godfather*.
His emissary, Apache tribe member Sacheen Littlefeather,
explained that Brando's rejection of the award was to protest
Hollywood's depiction of Native Americans. Backstage, John
Wayne was apoplectic. As John Lahr wrote in his article "The
Birth of the Oscar," "The Duke, who had dispatched many
an Apache on film, didn't take kindly to Brando's protest. . . .
Wayne had to be restrained by six men from yanking Little-
feather off the stage." *The New Yorker*, March 21, 1994.

For *Top Hat,* Irving Berlin's first movie score for Fred Astaire,
he seemed unable to write anything but hits, although nothing
surpasses "Cheek to Cheek," danced here by Astaire and
Ginger Rogers. "If Astaire had never existed," Wilfrid Sheed
wrote, "we might never have known how good Berlin was."
Illustration for Sheed's article "The Songwriters in Hollywood," *American Heritage,* October 1993.

In November 1924, while rehearsing *Lady Be Good* in Philadelphia, George Gershwin jumps up on stage and shows Fred Astaire how to conclude the "Fascinating Rhythm" number. Astaire takes his advice. From "Keyhole History," *GQ*, October 1984.

Wilfrid Sheed and I, both admirers of composer Harry Warren (who had even more songs on "The Hit Parade" than Irving Berlin), wished to pay him homage on the one hundredth anniversary of his birth. *The New Yorker* decided to humor us. Please humor me for thinking that my readers might want to see how a sketch develops into a finished work. Issue of December 20, 1993.

OPPOSITE:

The finish, as you see, has more scale. Going through their paces are Dick Powell, Ruby Keeler, and Warner Baxter, stars of the movie *Forty-second Street.*

Frank Sinatra has asked
Lauren Bacall (now Bogart's
widow) to marry him. While
out dining, a fan asks for
an autograph, and Sinatra
suggests she sign her new
name. She writes both on a
napkin—"Lauren Bacall"
followed by "Betty Sinatra."
The fact strikes home, and
Sinatra panics. It is a very
short engagement. From
"Scoundrel Time" by
Nancy Caldwell Sorel, *GQ,*
June 1986.

OPPOSITE:
New York magazine needed
a tiny black-and-white spot
of Frank Sinatra. Nothing
to get nervous about, and
therefore easy to do a really
good drawing.

This is a drawing of Barbra Streisand. I can't remember when I did it, who I did it for, or what it's supposed to mean, but it's definitely Barbra Streisand.

OPPOSITE:
Back in the mid-sixties, my friend George Lois had an idea for an *Esquire* cover that couldn't be done with photography. He asked me to do it, and I panicked—i.e., I tightened up. When I handed him my finish, he rolled his eyes and said he'd give me until the next morning to do it over. I went beyond panic, but nevertheless did a drawing we were both happy with. *Esquire,* April 1966.

70

Edward Sorel
(WITH APOLOGIES TO PIERRE AUGUSTE COT)

First act *Sturm,* second act *Drang.* Drawing for the "Artist's Notebook," *The New Yorker,* April 19, 1993.

OPPOSITE:
Pierre Auguste Cot is remembered for only one painting, *The Storm,* which seemed a good metaphor for Woody Allen and Mia Farrow. Illustration for a review of Allen's movie *Husbands and Wives* in *Rolling Stone,* October 1992.

Satyrs weren't meant to be husbands, as Olga Koklova was forced to conclude of Picasso. "Let's Call the Whole Thing Off," *GQ,* July 1988.

OPPOSITE:
In 1979 I did a Spring Book List spoof for *Esquire.* One entry was "The Erotic Art of Norman Rockwell" by A. H. Ginzburg. Here Rockwell finishes off a masterpiece of his "Blue Period." According to the reviewer, "This new direction may enhance Rockwell's reputation as a serious painter. It certainly can't hurt." *Esquire,* March 13, 1979.

The revived *Vanity Fair* of the early 1980s was a far different magazine from the one we know today. An article on the composer Verdi would have no place in the magazine's present incarnation. This illustration was for "Viva Verdi! The Story of a Love Affair" by Walter Clemons. Cherubs approach with a portrait of Verdi's wife, Giuseppina, as Maria Callas places a wreath on his head, Carlo Bergonzi sings, and Toscanini conducts the proceedings. Tito Gobbi as Falstaff stands lower right. *Vanity Fair*, June 1983.

Another drawing for Wilfrid Sheed's "The Songwriters in Hollywood." Top row: Dorothy Fields, E. Y. ("Yip") Harburg, George Gershwin, Ira Gershwin, Leo Robin, Richard Whiting, Johnny Mercer. Bottom row: Jerome Kern, Irving Berlin, Harry Warren, Richard Rodgers, Lorenz Hart, Cole Porter, Harold Arlen. *American Heritage,* October 1993.

OPPOSITE:
Duke Ellington and his Washingtonians were part of my pictorial essay celebrating the seventieth anniversary of *The New Yorker.* The drummer on the left is Sonny Greer. *The New Yorker,* February 20, 1995.

For an issue of *The New Yorker* devoted to the Academy Awards, I drew the "walls of Jericho" scene from *It Happened One Night* with Claudette Colbert and Clark Gable. March 21, 1994. Below: Leslie Howard, drawn for an article "The Making of *Gone With the Wind*," *Atlantic Monthly*, February 1973.

Ashley

OPPOSITE:
My caption for this cartoon about Ginger Rogers was "And I've always been careful about my diet. In fact, without make-up on I weigh exactly what I did when I made *Flying Down to Rio.*" *Village Voice*, October 11, 1976.

Victor McLaglen, Joseph Sauers (Sawyer), Preston Foster,
and Heather Angel in a scene from *The Informer* (1935).
From my series "Movie Classics," *Esquire,* November 1981.

OPPOSITE:
"The Music Man," an autobiographical strip for my monthly
page in *The Nation,* March 30, 1992.

JUST BECAUSE I'M IMPATIENT WITH FRIENDS WHO DON'T KNOW HOW TO SAY "GOODBYE"...

...AND I'M NO GOOD AT HIDING MY BOREDOM WHEN FRIENDS GO ON AND ON ABOUT THEIR PROBLEMS...

...AND BECAUSE I HATE PHYSICAL DEMONSTRATIONS OF AFFECTION— ESPECIALLY FROM MEN...

...PEOPLE SEE ME AS A COLD FISH...SELF-ABSORBED AND UNFEELING.

YET AT THE MOVIES I CRY AT ANYTHING SENTIMENTAL OR INSPIRATIONAL...

...AND AT MUSICALS I ALWAYS CRY AT THE FINALE WHEN THE LOVERS ARE REUNITED...

...I EVEN CRY AT THE COMMERCIAL WHERE THE MUSIC SWELLS AND THEN THE SON TELEPHONES HIS MOTHER.

IF ONLY REAL LIFE HAD MOOD MUSIC IN THE BACKGROUND TO TELL ME WHAT TO FEEL...

...THEN YOU'D SEE WHAT A WARM, CARING PERSON I REALLY AM.

Drawing of Louis Auchin-
closs for his article "The
Ten Greatest Business
Novels." The fact that stock
quotations are now elec-
tronic rather than the old
ticker tape has deprived
cartoonists of yet another
shorthand symbol.
Audacity, Summer 1993.

OPPOSITE:
Cover art, "Norman Rush
contemplates the bust of
socialism . . . and why we
all miss it so much." Every
caricaturist does at least one
parody of Rembrandt's
*Aristotle Contemplating the
Bust of Homer. The Nation,*
January 24, 1994.

Jerzy Kosinski visits the dying to give them solace by reading from his Holo-caust novels. From "Jews" by Alfred Kazin, *The New Yorker*, March 7, 1994.

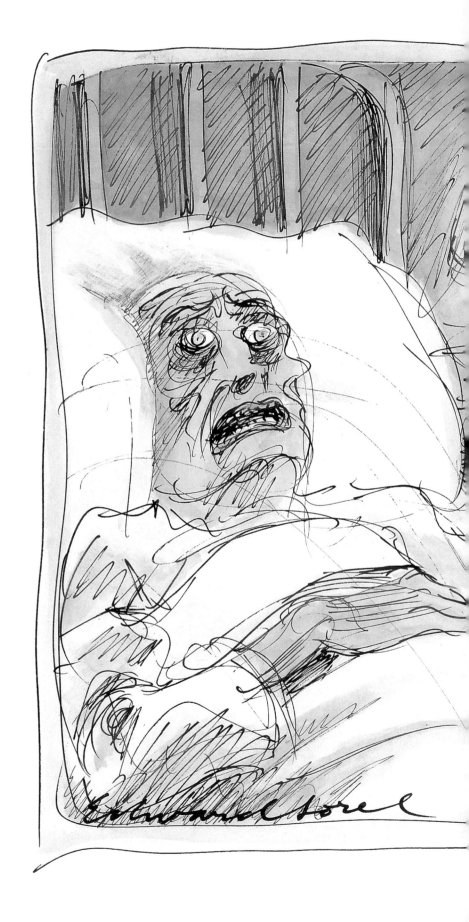

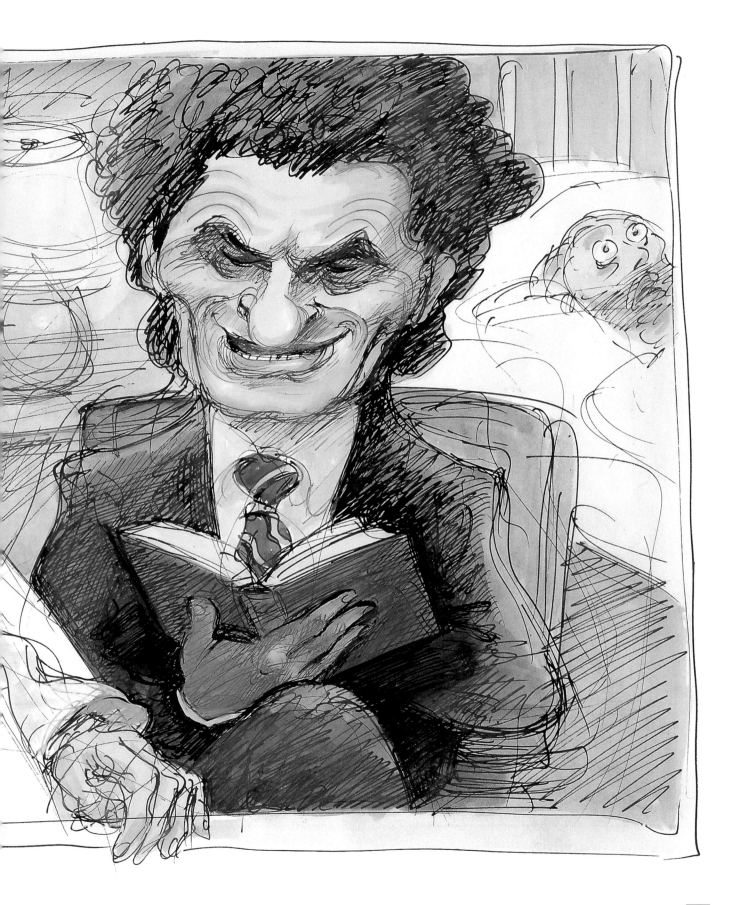

Noël Coward's most admired creation was always himself. He inaugurated two styles of dress—the dark turtleneck jersey (hitherto worn only by longshoremen) and elegant at-home wear. Personally, I'm something of a slob, but any man who loves art deco is my kind of guy. From my pictorial essay "Fashion Plates," *GQ,* December 1996.

OPPOSITE:
Tom Wolfe is a pretty good cartoonist himself. He also writes. But for my article "Fashion Plates," it was his white suits that intrigued me. Wolfe rebuts the charge that he is a fop. On the contrary, he insists, the proper term for a man like himself is "counterbohemian." *GQ,* December 1996.

Bennett Cerf was one of the names used by the Famous Writers School to lure students into signing up for a mail-order course. It was absurd to believe that any of the celebrated faculty actually corrected the students' papers, but if Cerf had, it would be such a scene as this. Done for *New York* magazine.

OPPOSITE:
Director Michael Blakemore, at a rehearsal of Woody Allen's one-act contribution to *Death Defying Acts,* watches in horror as Allen scribbles copious stage directions for him to execute. (Caricaturing Woody Allen is so easy that after drawing him, many an amateur comes to think of himself as a pro.) From Blakemore's "Death Defying Director," *The New Yorker,* June 3, 1996.

For their "*Forbes* 400" issue, the editors asked me to do a story on the portrayal of wealthy men in the movies of the 1930s, assuming that they were depicted in an unflattering way. On the contrary, I found that especially during the Depression era, these men were invariably shown as victims rather than oppressors, beset by inconsiderate workers and unreasonable unions. Five actors had a near monopoly on playing Hollywood's stereotypical millionaires: (left to right) Edward Arnold, Eugene Pallette, Roland Young, Charles Coburn, and Walter Connolly. From "Top Hat, White Tie, and Lovable," *Forbes*, October 28, 1985.

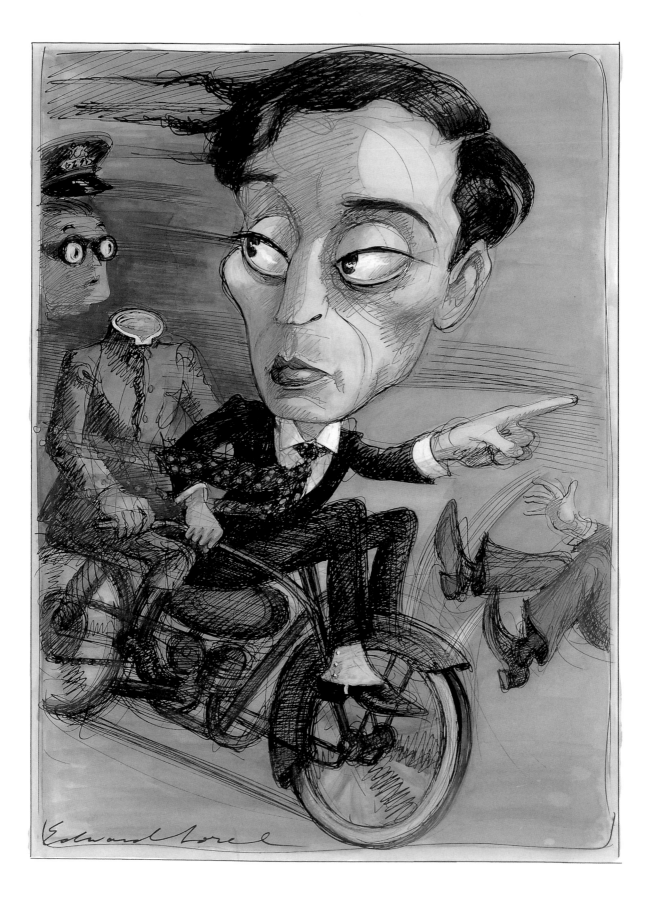

The General, starring Buster Keaton, is the only silent movie I included in my "Movie Classics" series. Based on an actual incident in the Civil War, it often has the look of a Mathew Brady photograph. *Esquire,* December 1980.

OPPOSITE:
Buster Keaton in a hurry, from a job done in a hurry for the movie listings in *The New Yorker,* March 13, 1995.

OVERLEAF:
"The Warner Mob": (left to right) George Raft, Humphrey Bogart, Eduardo Ciannelli, Jack Warner, James Cagney, Barton MacLane, Edward G. Robinson, and John Garfield. For the never-realized *New York Film Review,* 1977.

Trapped inside a brewery, a terrified Peter Lorre stands accused before a tribunal of criminals in *M,* an early (1931) German talkie about a psychotic child-murderer. It's the movie in which director Fritz Lang gave full expression to a theme he would return to often: the agony of a helplessly trapped victim. Although this drawing is one of my favorites from the "Movie Classics" series, its duplication of the actual movie still proved to me that I, too, was "a helplessly trapped victim"— trapped by the iconographic force of the film scenes themselves. Unable to free myself, I brought the series to an end. *Esquire,* August 1980.

My friend Jim McMullan's posters for Lincoln Center Theater are without peer, so when I was called in twice, I assumed these were productions he had turned down. (He denies it.) *Some Americans Abroad* was a comedy about academics escorting their students around London. The English playwright did not present his subjects in a flattering light. Shakespeare and Shaw had nothing to do with the play, but they say "England" to everyone, and they're easy to draw.

My other shot at theater immortality was for Spalding Gray's *Monster in a Box.* This time I opted for pastels, and wish I hadn't. Pastel just isn't as funny as line.

OVERLEAF:
Book jacket for Hugh Kenner's *A Colder Eye: The Modern Irish Writers.* This was my first attempt at pastels. The first mistake I made was to start on the right-hand side, which is not smart for a right-handed person. I intended to caricature my subjects, but after Joyce, they became more and more naturalistic. From right to left, as I did them: James Joyce, W. B. Yeats, Sean O'Casey, Samuel Beckett, Lady Gregory, Oliver St. John Gogarty, and J. M. Synge.

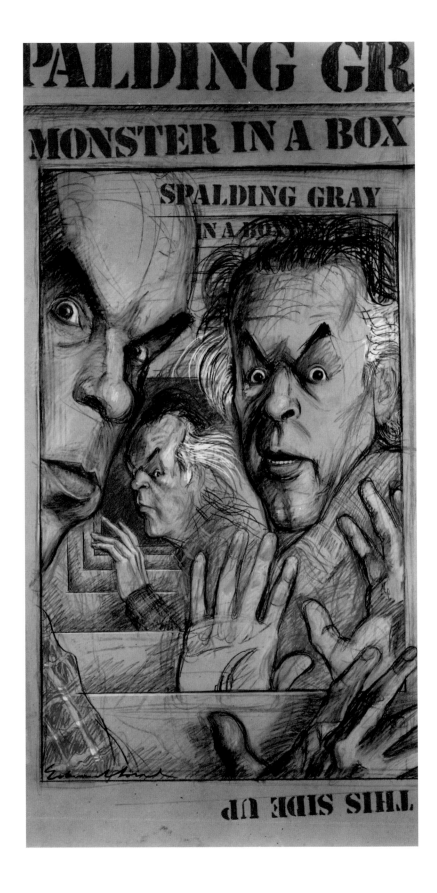

I TOOK MOM TO SEE DAVID LEVINE'S CARICATURES. SHE SAID, "I SUPPOSE HE'S GOOD, BUT BELIEVE ME EDDIE, HIS DRAWINGS JUST DON'T GET THE EXPRESSIONS THAT YOURS DO."

THEN WE WALKED TO A RESTAURANT AND SHE ASKED ME WHAT NANCY AND I WERE DOING. I TOLD HER THAT WE HAD GONE TO A DINNER HONORING JULES FEIFFER.

AND MOM SAID, "YES, I KNOW EVERYBODY SAYS HE'S VERY CLEVER, BUT LET'S FACE IT, EDDIE, AN ARTIST LIKE YOU HE'LL NEVER BE."

MOM ASKED IF I HAD SEEN THE FILM ABOUT SENDAK. I SAID I HAD, AND IN FACT HAD SEEN SENDAK HIMSELF THE NIGHT HE WAS INAUGURATED INTO THE ILLUSTRATORS' HALL OF FAME.

AND MOM SAID, "I'M SURE HE DESERVES IT, BUT TO TELL THE TRUTH, I NEVER SAW ANY BOOK HE DID THAT WAS AS BEAUTIFUL AS YOUR GWENDOLYN THE MIRACLE HEN."

I ALWAYS FEEL GREAT AFTER MY DINNER WITH MOM.

Politics

MY FIRST POLITICAL statement took place in 1938 in the auditorium of P.S. 88. The third grade had been taken there to enjoy a one-man magic show. Five minutes into his act, the magician pulled out of a hat a large silk square with a big red dot in the center. I perceived it to be the flag of Japan and instinctively began to boo. To my surprise, my fellow third graders joined in. The poor man, nonplussed, sputtered that it was an ice-skating flag, but he never quite regained his composure.

As one might gather, my family—my extended family—was very political. We were Jews, and Fascism seemed to be everywhere. Half my family were Communists and the other half wished that just once we could all get together without talking politics. I remember a lot of yelling. My tendency to draw pictures by myself in a corner was perhaps an attempt to escape all that conflict.

As I grew older, I discovered you didn't have to yell—you could ridicule. Humor was to me a much more comfortable means of expressing my opposition, and to that end I wrote and illustrated two small books: *How to Be President* (1960) and *Moon Missing* (1963). *Moon* came out on the first day of New York's long newspaper strike, and the half-page ad in the *Times* with quotes from people like Ben Shahn and Margaret Halsey never appeared. I found it a difficult matter to be philosophical about.

It was around then that I moved into the underground—and poverty-stricken overground—press. *Ramparts, The Realist,* the *National Lampoon,* the *Village Voice,* and later *The Nation* gave me space, both physically and intellectually. For a while I was syndicated with King Features, but their subscribers dumped me when I portrayed Richard Nixon juggling skulls. During the Vietnam era I played hardball; in succeeding years I valued subtlety more. The following section includes examples of both; the later pieces are drawn better, but I sometimes miss the intensity of that earlier time.

OPPOSITE:
"He has his mother's deep moral integrity, and in this sense I would call him basically devout" (Rev. Ezra Ellis, Pastor of First Friends Meeting, Whittier, California). From a personal collection of flattering quotes on Richard Nixon gathered during his presidency. *New York,* August 12, 1974.

Book jacket for Robert Scheer's *Thinking Tuna Fish, Talking Death: Essays on the Pornography of Power* (Hill & Wang, 1988). The idea was turned down by the publisher as being obscene, but the author insisted it be used. That fat man between Reagan and Gorbachev is Edwin Meese, Reagan's attorney general, now largely forgotten.

LBJ and Lady Bird in front of the Federal District Courthouse in Fort Worth. Cover illustration for the *Washington Post Book World,* March 4, 1990, accompanying a review of Robert Caro's *Means of Ascent,* volume 2 of his biography of Lyndon Johnson, in which Caro charges Johnson with stealing the 1948 senatorial election in Texas.

OPPOSITE:
A strip done for *The Nation* to celebrate the fiftieth anniversary of V-E Day.

LBJ as Icarus. For Nicholas Lemann's article "The Unfinished War," *Atlantic Monthly,* January 1989. The ill-fated War on Poverty was Johnson's great crusade until the one in Vietnam depleted the U.S. Treasury.

OPPOSITE:
Poster, in crayon and watercolor, of Cardinal Spellman going over the top in Vietnam (parody of a well-known World War I poster). Although opposition to the war had reached a crescendo by 1967, no magazine would publish this. It was made into a poster instead, but the day it came off the press, the cardinal died. It was never sold in this country, but is part of the collection of the Stedelijk Museum in Amsterdam.

Pass the Lord and
PRAISE THE AMMUNITION

A wounded LBJ returning from the War on Poverty, supported by Daniel Patrick Moynihan, adviser on urban affairs, and Sargent Shriver, head of the Office of Economic Opportunity, and greeted by Columbia with a needy American child in her arms. Illustration for "The Unfinished War" by Nicholas Lemann, *Atlantic Monthly*, January 1989.

On my first *Time* magazine
cover, Mario Procaccino,
mayoral candidate, leads the
blue-collar revolt against
bleeding-heart liberals in
New York City. Mayor John
V. Lindsay views his oppo-
nent anxiously, while former
mayor Robert F. Wagner Jr.
is well out of it. Lindsay eked
out a narrow victory after all.

OPPOSITE:
This bipolar portrait of
Mayor John V. Lindsay
portrayed him both as a
"Red" (as the right wing saw
him) and as an accommodat-
ing politician (my view).
Illustration for an article on
"How Moscow Views New
York" by "Adam Smith,"
New York, July 13, 1970.

FROM EACH ACCORDING
TO HIS ABILITY...
TO EACH ACCORDING
TO HIS GREED

One of a series of movie-poster parodies I did annually for *New York* magazine. My copy read in part: "Mile-high spectacle with suspense on every floor! David Rockefeller gives his usual suave performance as a banker who builds the city's tallest buildings only to discover nobody wants to rent floor space there. But—clever plot—his brother turns out to be governor, and all ends happily when hundreds of state agencies are moved in and the bank's investment is secure." *New York*, December 29, 1975.

OPPOSITE:
Rupert Murdoch as the blood-sucking fiend Dracula. Cover illustration for the article "Murdoch Stalks Chicago," *Columbia Journalism Review*, May–June 1984.

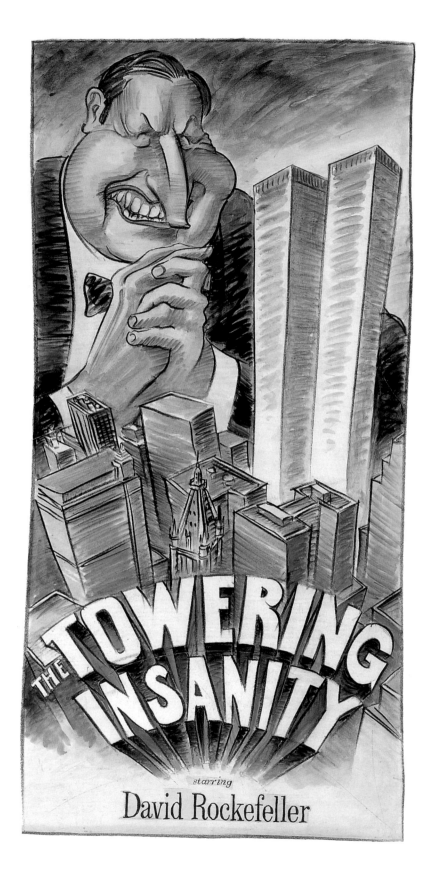

During his 1962 campaign for governor of California, Nixon
was asked repeatedly about the secret $200,000 loan defense
contractor Howard Hughes had made to his brother Donald.
Here, dining in San Francisco's Chinatown, he opens a
fortune cookie to discover the message, "What About the
Hughes Loan?"—a joke arranged by a Democratic political
prankster. From "Footnotes to History," *American Heritage,*
February 1990.

OPPOSITE:
"Après moi le déluge!" Richard Nixon as Louis XVI,
Washington Post Book World, August 5, 1973.

"Milhous I," Richard Nixon as Lord of San Clemente, Duke of Key Biscayne, and Captain of Watergate. Illustration for an article by Richard Goodwin for *Rolling Stone,* March 14, 1974.

OPPOSITE:
The artist drawn and quartered by his subjects (and himself). Cover illustration for Steven Heller's article "A Political Animal," *Print* magazine (January–February 1993). Although much of this issue concentrated on my work, many readers wrote in to ask who that was posing on the cover.

Spiro Agnew in a parody
of yet another World War I
poster. From an article in
Harper's by Kirkpatrick Sale
and myself.

OPPOSITE:
Spiro Agnew as George
Washington, "First in War,
First in Peace, First in the
Hearts of His Country
Club." *Atlantic Monthly*.

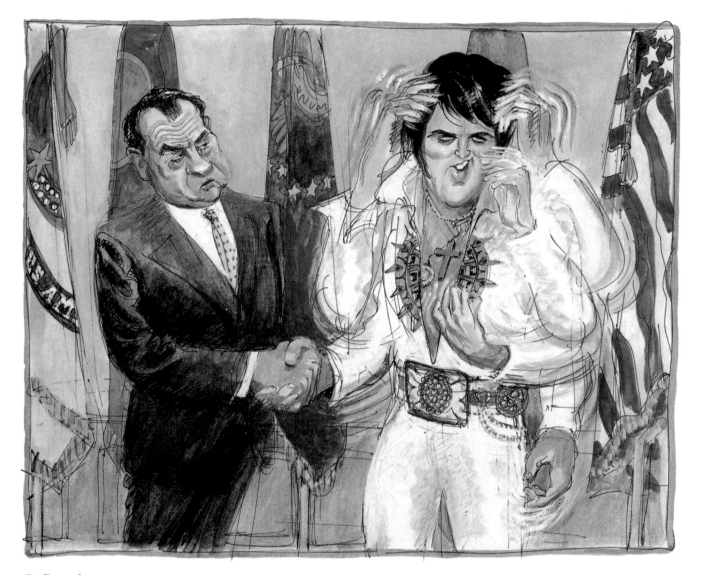

On December 21, 1970, President Nixon appointed Elvis Presley a special agent of the Bureau of Narcotics in a ceremony marred only by Elvis's incessant scratching of his skin due to a drug-related condition. From "Keyhole History," *GQ*, October 1984.

OPPOSITE:
And while we're on the subject of Elvis—his deification after death inspired this cartoon. I take no responsibility for later versions of this idea. *Penthouse*, December 1992.

"The Watergate Shoot-Out" appeared in *Ramparts*, June 1972, more than two years before Richard Nixon was forced to resign from the presidency. Once again my obsession with 1930s movies inspired me. Watergate reminded me of those melodramas where the trapped gang leader says, "Come and get me, copper!" This gang includes (clockwise from Nixon) James McCord, Jeb Magruder, John Ehrlichman, Patrick Gray, Richard Kleindienst, Maurice Stans, John Mitchell, H. R. Haldeman, and, center, John Dean.

This is my very favorite movie-poster parody, perhaps because it proved clairvoyant: it appeared some months before Gerald Ford actually did grant Nixon a presidential pardon. *New York,* April 15, 1974.

OPPOSITE:
My wife says I have no right to be outraged that Billy Graham feels himself appointed to speak for God since I don't believe in God. But I am anyway. *Penthouse,* June 1992.

As the fifth anniversary of the Watergate break-in approached, I imagined the old gang, dressed in lederhosen, gathering for a reunion. Viewed clockwise from John Ehrlichman, in left foreground: Donald Segretti, Richard Kleindienst, Jeb Magruder, James Mc-Cord, Howard Hunt (in Tyrolean cap), John Dean, G. Gordon Liddy (waving), Charles Colson, Rosemary Woods, H. R. Haldeman, and John Mitchell.
Penthouse, July 1977.

An illustration for Roy Blount Jr.'s satirical essay "Forgiveness Is the Best Revenge." Blount is ready to forgive the shameless sleazebags who have been caught sinning in the past year if they will only confess their evil deeds. Sinners include (left to right) Michael Milken, Ivan Boesky, Leona Helmsley, Pete Rose, Oliver North, Richard Nixon, Rob Lowe, Jimmy Swaggert, and Jim and Tammy Bakker. *Special Report,* August–October 1990.

Three politicians who never came clean are Nelson Rockefeller, Gerald Ford, and Henry Kissinger. I can no longer remember whom I drew this for.

This portrait of Henry Kissinger is a swipe from Daumier's *Narcissus*. It appeared in the *Washington Post Book World*, illustrating the Secretary of State's memoirs, *White House Years*, reviewed by Townsend Hoopes, November 25, 1979.

OPPOSITE:
More swiping. Gustave Doré did this first, without Dr. K. For Garry Wills's "Kissinger Triumphant," referring to the sovereign schemer who somehow managed to turn each defeat into a personal victory. *GQ*, December 1983.

Time cover of Jimmy Carter in the lion's den. *Time* magazine always portrayed Republican presidents as wise and powerful and Democratic presidents as naïve and vacillating. I preferred to see Jimmy Carter as well-intentioned. Here he is surrounded by wily beasts: (counterclockwise) Helmut Schmidt, Mao, Anwar Sadat, Mcnachcm Begin, and Leonid Brezhnev. *Time,* August 8, 1977.

OPPOSITE:
"I, Odious." When movie prices were raised in New York City, Mayor Ed Koch, an inveterate moviegoer, threatened to take legal action. He was not similarly galvanized by the city's other problems. *The Nation,* January 30, 1988.

Ronald Reagan as Robin Hood shaking down the poor for the benefit of the rich. Illustration for a review of *Sleepwalking Through History: America in the Reagan Years,* by Haynes Johnson (color added later). *Washington Post Book World,* February 24, 1991.

OPPOSITE:
The public's disillusionment with Ed Koch and Ronald Reagan occurred at much the same time. I imagined what might happen if they encountered each other in a bar. *The Nation,* January 31, 1987.

Visualizing Ronald Reagan's first summit with Mikhail Gorbachev, at Reykjavík, Iceland. *Village Voice,* November 26, 1985.

Lieutenant Ronald Reagan, stationed in Culver City, California, in 1942, wrote a monthly feature for *Modern Screen* magazine called "Dear Button Nose." It consisted of his letters home to his wife, Jane Wyman (whom he saw at home every night), describing what army life was like. "Keyhole History," *GQ*, October 1984.

OPPOSITE:
Titled "1984." Reagan's hold on the concept of democratic safeguards always seemed to me tenuous at best. *The Nation*, October 20, 1984.

The Jesse Jackson family
at home. Illustration for
an article entitled "An
American Family" by
Marshall Frady, *The New
Yorker,* April 29, 1996.

OPPOSITE:
Cover illustration for an
article on the Democratic
convention of 1988.
Michael Dukakis led in
the polls for about three
minutes afterward.
*Columbia Journalism
Review,* September–
October 1988.

George Bush introducing
vice presidential candidate
J. Danforth Quayle at the
1988 Republican convention,
as a representative of a new
generation of Americans.
GQ, May 1989.

OPPOSITE:
"Résumé." George Bush's
chief campaign thrust was
that he had experience
and Bill Clinton didn't. To
me it seemed that it was this
very experience that dis-
qualified him. *The Nation*,
November 2, 1992.

"Dependence Day, 1993."
It often seemed to me that
Robert Dole confused his
loyalty to American corpo-
rate structure—Philip Mor-
ris, Dow Chemical, Archer
Daniels Midland, etc.—with
loyalty to America. *The
Nation,* July 19, 1993.

OPPOSITE:
In 1989 I began a series in
GQ magazine called "The
Adventures of J. Danforth."
I felt a certain sympathy
for Quayle; my own father
didn't think I was very bright
either. *GQ,* June 1989.

Uncle Sam consoling Newt Gingrich, who had suggested a tax credit "for the poorest Americans to buy a laptop" so they could be part of the "third-wave information age," forgetting that the poorest Americans pay no taxes to have a credit against. But perhaps they will next year. From my pictorial essay "A Short-Form History of Taxation," *GQ*, March 1996.

OPPOSITE:
"Political Descent '96," cover illustration for *The Nation*, November 4, 1996.

"Difficult Days Ahead."
Every time a new President
comes along, I worry about
what to exaggerate. With
Richard Nixon I had noth-
ing to worry about. *The
Nation*, February 1, 1993.

OPPOSITE:
"Inaugural Address 1993."
I assumed Clinton would
speak too long as usual (note
Teddy Roosevelt at right),
but in fact his talk was one of
the shortest on record.
Cover illustration, *The New
Yorker*, January 25, 1993.
Please don't write asking me
to identify all the presidents.

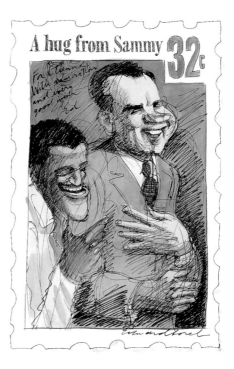

When Richard Nixon died in
1994, the U.S. Postal Service,
following custom, issued a
commemorative stamp, a
properly heroic portrait by
my friend Daniel Bennett
Schwartz. These would have
been my submissions, had I
been asked. *The New Yorker,*
April 24, 1995.

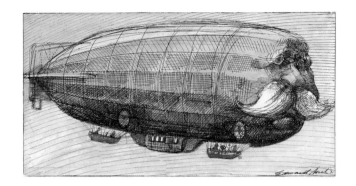

A Note on the Type

This book was set in a typeface called Bulmer. This distinguished letter is a replica of a type long famous in the history of English printing which was designed and cut by William Martin about 1790 for William Bulmer of the Shakespeare Press. In design, it is all but a modern face, with vertical stress, sharp differentiation between the thick and thin strokes, and nearly flat serifs. The decorative italic shows the influence of Baskerville, as Martin was a pupil of John Baskerville's.

Composed by North Market Street Graphics,
Lancaster, Pennsylvania
Color separations, printing, and binding by
Arnoldo Mondadori Editore S.p.A., Verona, Italy
Designed by Marcus Ratliff